Leopards on Mars

Leopards on Mars

Richard Edwards

Illustrated by Sarah Jane Stewart

VIKING

VIKING

Published by the Penguin Group
Penguin Books Ltd, 27 Wrights Lane, London w8 5tz, England
Penguin Books USA Inc., 375 Hudson Street, New York, New York 10014, USA
Penguin Books Australia Ltd., Ringwood, Victoria, Australia
Penguin Books Canada Ltd, 10 Alcorn Avenue, Toronto, Ontario, Canada m4v 3b2
Penguin Books (NZ) Ltd, 182–190 Wairau Road, Auckland 10, New Zealand

Penguin Books Ltd, Registered Offices: Harmondsworth, Middlesex, England

First published 1993
10 9 8 7 6 5 4 3 2 1
First edition

Filmset in 12/14pt Linotype Plantin
by Rowland Phototypesetting Ltd,
Bury St Edmunds, Suffolk
Made and printed in Great Britain by
Butler and Tanner Ltd, Frome and London

A CIP catalogue record for this book is available from the British Library

ISBN 0–670–83821–7

Contents

Leopards on Mars

Nothing lives on Mars – too hot,
Too dried up, too seared a spot,
Nothing lives on Mars, except the leopards.

Martian leopards – ember-red;
No gazelles, chase dust instead,
Nothing lives on Mars, except the leopards.

Martian leopards – white-hot claws,
Burning eyes, volcano roars,
Nothing lives on Mars, except the leopards.

Martian leopards, playing games,
Jumping smoke and biting flames,
Nothing lives on Mars, except the leopards.

Martian leopards, thin as wire;
Hunger blazing like a fire,
Nothing lives on Mars, except the leopards.

Martian leopards, hear them pray:
'Send an astronaut one day,
Send one astronaut, send two,
Bones for me and fat for you.'
Nothing lives on Mars, except the leopards.

Mac Mac

Mac Mac woke up at seven
And combed his hairy chin,
Mac Mac went out
And searched about
For mud to wallow in.

Mac Mac came to a puddle
And tried it with his toe,
But shook his head,
'No good,' he said,
'Too shallow, much too low.'

Mac Mac came to a duck-pond,
All gummed and scummed with ooze,
A mucky sight,
The mud just right,
Mac Mac kicked off his shoes.

He paddled to his ankles,
He waded to his chest,
He squealed to feel
A friendly eel
Exploring in his vest.

He writhed, he rolled, he wriggled,
He soaped himself with grime,
And ducks went quack
As happy Mac
Sank deeper in the slime.

And later, as the moonlight
Shone down on Mac Mac's head,
He blew a spout
Of mud, squelched out
And slithered home to bed.

An Appetite for Words

There are books about castles
And countries and cats,
There are books about kings and canoeing.
There are books about battles
And badgers and bats,
There are books about bridges and brewing.
There are books about horses
And history and hats,
There are books about trees and tattooing,
And I like them all,
Fact, fiction, big, small,
Said the rat in the library vault, chewing.

The Green Bear

I am a green bear.

I do not dig a den like other bears,
Instead I build
A nest in a tree,
And climb to it at dusk,
And lie there while the mild winds
Rock me to sleep.

I am a green bear.

I do not eat berries or fish like other bears,
Instead I eat
Loaves of earth,
Which I set in the sun to dry
Until they're crunchy on the outside,
Sticky in.

I am a green bear.

I do not roar or snarl like other bears,
Instead I sing,
On moon-dark nights,
A short song
Like the foggy whistle
Of a distant train.

I am a green bear.

I am the colour of grass,
If I lay down in a field
You could walk
Straight by,
And not even know I was there.
It happens often.

I am a green bear.

I have green fur and a green
Heart and green
Meat on green
Bones, and I ask myself this question:
Am I the last in a long line of green bears,
Or am I, perhaps, the first?

I am a green bear.

Bubbling Over

'Luxuro-foam,' the label said,
'The best foam-bath there is.'
I bought some, poured some, turned the taps
And watched the bubbles fizz.
I nipped out of the bathroom
To fetch some clean pyjamas,
And when I tried to get back in,
The foam had gone bananas.

An overflowing mountain
Of glitter, froth and air,
It seethed out of the bathroom door
And chased me down the stair.
A snowy, oozy foam-drift,
Advancing like the tide,
It filled my house from rug to roof,
From side to soapy side.

My house is bubbling over –
I'm lathered through and through,
There's lather in the cupboard drawers
And lather down the loo.
I'm sunk in glug, engulfed in suds,
Nose-deep in gurgling troubles,
Deliver me! Oh, set me free!
Unbubble me from bubbles!

I Said to the Ant

I said to the ant:
'My leg's a mountain,
Climb it to the knee
And you can stick in a flag
To celebrate your conquest
Of the peak.'

The ant was too ambitious.
It passed my knee
And went on up,
And started to explore
Where it should not.

I squashed it.

Let this be a lesson to all ants.

Ice in the Wind

Ice in the wind, storm-thrashed heather,
A voice, 'Come in out of this wild weather.'
A round stone hut on the empty moor,
A creaking hinge, an opening door.

Smoke from a fire, a low domed room,
A baby coughing, faces in the gloom,
Sparks at the hearth, a lifted brand,
A bowl that steamed in an outstretched hand.

I shook my head. I could not stay.
'I've lost the path.' 'Go west a way.'
A nod, a smile, the door again,
Out into the dusk and the pelt of rain.

Ice in the wind, storm-thrashed heather,
No relief from the worsening weather,
Just bare hills and me, alone,
Standing by a heap of tumbled stone.

Hallowe'en Sandwiches

Sandwiches for Ghosts

Take two long shadows
Butter with dust
Fill with gooseflesh

Sandwiches for Witches

Take two dried bats' wings
Butter with toadfat
Fill with curses

Sandwiches for Vampires

Take some 'Type A'
Butter with 'Type B'
Fill with 'O'

Busking Bertie

Round the round world Bertie went,
Rhyming place and instrument,

So, on tour in Mexico,
Bertie played the piccolo,

Then drove down to hot Caracas,
Where he rattled hot maracas,

Flew to tropical Rangoon,
Serenaded on bassoon,

Travelled northwards to Tibet,
Blew some blues on clarinet,

Moved to Europe, liked Turin,
Stayed and bowed his violin,

Headed west to grey Cologne,
Busked the squares on saxophone,

France was next and chic Bordeaux
Echoed to his twanged banjo,

Crossed the seas to Panama,
Played jazz on a cool guitar,

Then one day in sunny Cuba,
As he oompahed on the tuba,

Suddenly he lost his puff.
'Right,' said Bertie. 'That's enough,

All this rhyming stuff must stop!'
Sold his tuba to a shop.

Caught a jumbo jet to Venice,
Took up tennis.

One Safe Place

There's only one safe place:
It isn't up a tree
It isn't in the wardrobe
Or under the stairs
Or behind the boxes in the shed
With the spiders.

There's only one safe place:
It isn't under the bed
It isn't behind the curtains
Or up in the loft
Or in the cold, rubbly passage
Next to the garage.

There's only one safe place:
It isn't in the long grass
It isn't behind the sofa
Or in the bathroom
Or curled up tightly, tightly
Under the duvet.

There's only one safe place.
There's only one safe place.

Where Are the Bones?

'Oh, where are the bones I left below?'
Cried the starved crow, quartering over the snow,
'Oh, where are the bones I left below?'
Cried the starved crow, searching the snow.

'Oh, whose are these bones that smell so nice?'
Said the fox, digging down through a crust of ice,
'Oh, whose are these bones that smell so nice?'
And he munched them once and he crunched them
    twice,
Till hardly a scrap was left to show
Of the bones the crow had left below,
Of the bare bones under the snow.

A Little Song

I caught a little goldfinch
And I tied its little leg
With a little piece of cotton
To a little wooden peg,
And it did a little singing
Till another finch flew down
Which I netted and I pocketed
To sell back in the town.

And I walked a little homewards
When I heard a little sound
As a big hand out of nowhere
Came and pinned me to the ground,
And I felt a little frightened
As it tied my little leg
With a little piece of cotton
To a little wooden peg.

Then I think I must have fainted
For the next thing that I heard
Was a little cage door closing
On me, changed into a bird,
And my little body trembled
From its feet to little head
When a voice came through the little bars:
'Sing!' it said.

In a Rock Pool

In a rock pool
At the foot of a harbour wall
In New England,
Two crabs were wrestling
For an audience of shrimps.

Up in the ring,
The referee,
A lobster,
Was getting worried.
For almost an hour
One Boston crab
Had had the other Boston crab
In a Boston crab
While the other Boston crab
Had had the first Boston crab
In a Boston crab
Too.

Stalemate.

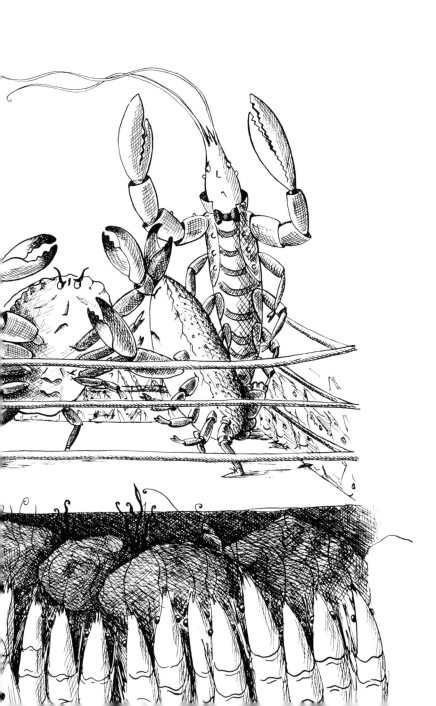

A Crime to Report

I've a crime to report –
The rowan-tree said –
The theft of some berries,
Small, round, red.
It happened this morning –
Kids, I suppose –
I was tired from the gale
And having a doze.

A difficult case –
The policeman said,
Licking his pencil
And scratching his head –
We'll send down forensics
To search for clues:
Fingerprints, tyre marks,
The imprint of shoes,
But, if you ask me,
This berrying job
Sounds like the work
Of the Mistle Thrush mob.
We'll do what we can –
But a word to the wise –
Get some insurance,
And watch the skies.

Zuleika at Her Books

I do not sit square
Because I am not made to sit square,
Said the circle.

I do not roll
Because I am not made to roll,
Said the square.

We will never touch
Because we are not made to touch,
Said the parallel lines.

More is better than less,
That's all I know,
Said the plus sign.

Less is better than more,
That's all I know,
Said the minus sign.

Neither of you is much good
Without me,
Said the equals.

Stupid, said Zuleika,
Closing her books,
Going out into the garden,
To look for worms.

The Ant Said to Me

I've one foot with a blister on
And one sore at the tip
And one that's got a nasty twinge
And one that gives me gyp
And one foot with a splinter in
And one foot with a sprain,
But after seeing the millepede –
How can I complain?

The Alleyway

The alleyway is crooked,
The alleyway is damp,
The alleyway has corners,
Untouched by any lamp,
The alleyway has bats in
And ghosts and thieves and rats in,
So please don't make me
Please don't make me
Please don't make me
Please don't make me
Please don't make me walk the alleyway.

The alleyway is dirty,
The alleyway is mean,
You see things in the alleyway
You wish you'd never seen,
The alleyway has litter
And smells and broken glass,
And things like rags that flap to catch
Your ankles as you pass,
And slimy stuff you tread in
And everything I dread in,
So please don't make me
Please don't make me
Please don't make me
Please don't make me
Please don't make me
Please don't make me walk the alleyway.

Transports

All the larks were flying, except one,
The thinking lark was basking in the sun,
Inventing the helicopter.

All the swans were paddling, except one,
The thinking swan was basking in the sun,
Inventing the yacht.

All the moles were digging, except one,
The thinking mole was basking in the sun,
Inventing the Underground train.

All the whales were sounding, except one,
The thinking whale was basking in the sun,
Inventing the submarine.

All the dogs were running, except one,
The thinking dog was basking in the sun,
Inventing the wheel.

Last Visit to Auntie

I felt rough. My voice croaked.
'There's a frog in your throat,'
Said my aunt. 'I've a syrup for that,
Made last April, by me,
From an old recipe
Using goose-grease and garlic and fat.'

She filled up a large spoon
And she dosed me, and soon
I was holding the edge of the sink,
Feeling queasy inside,
When my mouth opened wide
And I waited and, what do you think?

Something moved in my mouth
And a green frog jumped out,
And another three frogs followed suit,
And hopped all round the floor
To be joined by four more
And a natterjack toad and a newt.

'Feeling better?' Aunt asked.
'Yes, I think so,' I gasped,
'Though I'm hoarse and my tongue's gone all
    slack.'
'Horse, you say?' Auntie cried,
'Where's that spoon? Open wide.'
So I ran, and I'm not going back.

Being Heard

Under an inch-thick
Pane of ice,
A goldfish looked up at me
From a frozen pond,
And opened its mouth.

Was it asking for help?
Or whispering a secret?

I knelt on the ice
And felt the cold burn
Against my ear.
'Speak,' I said.
The fish stared.
'Please speak.'
But the fish turned tail and slowly
Sank away
Into the depths.

On standing up,
I saw I had drawn a crowd.
Some shook their heads,
Some laughed,
One said something about calling the police;
And when I tried to explain,
I felt as small and as cold
As a goldfish
Under an inch-thick
Pane of ice,
Trying to make itself heard.

A Very Short Story

A man dressed as a bear
Walked into a bear's lair
And said, 'Hello, I want to be your friend.'
The hungry bear said, 'Fine,
I'm just about to dine.'
The man was never seen again.

The End.

There Isn't a Monkey in the Attic

Oh, yes, there is . . .

It wakes at nightfall.
It dances across the rafters.
It swings through the roofbeams, showing its teeth.

There isn't a monkey in the attic.

Oh, yes there is.
It hunts and feasts on spiders.
It drinks from the water-tank, lapping like a cat.
It pokes a finger through the roof insulation and
    scratches on the ceiling, pretending to be a
    ghost.

There isn't a monkey in the attic.

Oh, yes, there is.
It opens the box of comics and leafs through them.
It unclicks the suitcase of old photographs and has
    a good laugh.
It empties the trunk of Christmas decorations and
    dresses up in them, tinsel round its shoulders, a
    fairy on top of its head.

There isn't a monkey in the attic.

Oh, yes, there is.
It sleeps in a nest of newspapers, under a dust-
  sheet.
If you go up very quietly, you can hear its monkey
  snores,
You can smell its monkey smell.

There isn't a monkey in the attic.

Oh, yes, there is . . .

The Apple Says Goodbye to Its Tree

I've liked it here, high above the ground,
Bouncing in the breezes as the sun rolls round,
Growing from a bud to a blossom to a bump
Of green, to me now, ripe and plump
And good enough to eat. So, thanks, old tree,
For one long summer, carrying me,
But now it's time to leave. What waits beneath?
Some say deep sleep, some say teeth.
One way of finding out. Watch out below –
Here I come. Geronimo-o-o-o!

Maxo, the Magician

Maxo, the magician,
Was very sharp and slick,
And people flocked from miles around
To see his famous trick,
The one that conjured rabbits,
A hare, two ducks, a cat,
A dozen hens, three foxes
And a goat out of a hat.

Everyone loved Maxo,
They'd 'Bravo!' and applaud,
Yes, everyone loved Max, except
The hat, the hat was bored
And envious – it never got
A single cheer or clap,
And one night at the Hippodrome,
It felt its patience snap.

Maxo, the magician,
Had flashed his brilliant grin,
Had tapped the hat-brim with his wand,
Had started reaching in,
When something startling happened –
He screeched out in alarm,
His hand went in the hat, his wrist,
His elbow, his whole arm,

His cloaked-in-velvet shoulder,
And then, as people cheered,
His head, his chest, his legs and feet
Entirely disappeared.
The audience roared 'Maxo!
Oh, Maxo, sharp and slick,
He's made his whole self vanish
In the hat. Oh, what a trick!'

The curtain fell. The stage-hands
Searched everywhere in vain,
But Maxo, the magician,
Was never seen again.
His dressing-room stands silent now,
And dust lies in his hat,
Which sometimes makes a low
Digestive rumble. Fancy that!

Otter to Oyster, Prudhoe Bay

– Oyster, let me come inside,
It's dark out here, the poisoned tide
Is dimming. I can't see.

The oyster said nothing.

– Oyster, oyster, let me hide,
The black stuff's spreading thick and wide.
I'm choking. I can't breathe.

The oyster said nothing.

– Oyster, please . . . The otter sighed,
Rolled on to its back and died.
Overhead a seagull cried,

But the oyster said nothing.

47

A Tie's Too Tight

'A hat's a thing,' my uncle said,
'That people balance on their head.
A sock's a soft thing like a shoe,
That people stuff their toes into,
And long johns are, I think you'll find,
Designed to cover your behind,
But a tie, a tie's too tight.

'A scarf's a thing,' he wittered on,
'To heat you when September's gone,
And braces are quite useful, for
They hoist your trousers off the floor,
And shirts, unbuttoned mind, are just
The things to keep you free from dust,
But a tie, a tie's too tight.

'And ties were thought up by a fool,
Some say they're smart, I say they're cruel.
They chafe your neck, they pinch, they're bad,
They dangle like a tongue gone mad,
A tie's a strangling pest, a pain,
I'll never wear a tie again
Till blood runs green and snow falls red.'
('Oh, yes you will,' my auntie said.)

A Message for Hedgehogs

Keep away from goldfish ponds
And swimming-pools.
You may need to take a drink
From time to time,
Everybody needs a drink,
But look for dew
On a grass stem, or snuffle
Shallow puddles,
Or come to my step at night
And I'll put out
A bowl of sweet milk for you,
More than enough,
But keep away from fish ponds,
Or you'll end up
Like this – like the swollen husk
Of a chestnut
Lost to water. Goldfish ponds
And swimming-pools,
Avoid them carefully, give
Them a wide berth –
For your kind they're as cruel, as
Deadly as roads.

The Thing With a Feather

'Oh, where is the thing with a feather?'
Demanded the ticklish king,
'I've tried using bits of soft leather
And whiskery ends of frayed string.
I've tried thistle-heads
And the horsehair from beds,
But not even straw
Can make me guffaw,
So where is the thing with a feather?'

'Oh, here is the thing with a feather!'
A courtier said, rushing inside,
'I found it stuffed under some heather,
I'll soon have it fluffy and dried.'

And soon the thing flickered
And soon the king snickered
And then the thing wiggled
And then the king giggled
And laughed to the cuffs of his coat,

And laughed till he stumbled
And staggered and tumbled
And fell with a splash in the moat,
And that was the end of the ticklish king,
Who hadn't remembered this one simple thing:
That things with a feather –
Though ticklier than leather –
Don't float.

Only the Best

I breakfast on muesli,
I lunch on raw greens,
I dine on a potage of parsnips and beans.
I'm pure as spring water and healthier too.
(I long for a burger, a sausage, some stew,
I long for some sausage, some stew.)

I never touch fried things
Or full-fatted cheese,
I drink only fruit juice and honeyed herb teas.
I'm pure as spring water and healthier too.
(I long for a great slab of fudge cake to chew,
I long for some fudge cake to chew.)

I fast every Monday,
On Tuesdays a crunch
Of apple and carrot is all that I munch.
I'm pure as spring water and healthier too.
(Do you eat pink ice-cream mashed up in a goo?
You do? Oh, I wish I were you!
You do? How I wish I were you!)

The Wall That Walked

There once was a wall that walked –
Why not?
It got tired of standing in the same fixed spot,
So it walked.

There once was a wall that walked,
Or flowed,
Like a river of stone across the main road.
A policeman tried to arrest it,
But it made for his boots, so he left it alone
To walk.

There once was a wall that walked
Right through
Spain, France, Belgium and Italy too.
It rested in Germany, but people with picks
Came in the darkness and bashed at its bricks,
So it walked.

There once was a wall that walked
To China,
A nice quiet place, it couldn't think of one finer,
So it settled itself. And it's settled there still,
Draped like a rope over valley and hill,
Stretched like a wire, like a fast-asleep snake,
But some day soon now, the wall will awake,
And walk.

Crocodiles

Crocodiles, crocodiles, crocodiles, crocodiles,
Snapping whenever I dream,
Nothing but crocodiles, save me from crocodiles,
Take them away or I'll scream.

Crocodiles thrashing and crocodiles barging,
Crocodiles lashing the water and charging,
Crocodiles flying and climbing up trees,
Crocodiles talking in crocodilese,
Crocodiles dressed in suits, crocodiles nude,
Crocodiles shopping with trolleys for food,
Trains full of crocodiles, sheds full of crocodiles,
Baths full of crocodiles, beds full of crocodiles,
Crocodiles walking in crocodile file,
Crocodile crocodiles, mile after mile . . .

Crocodiles, crocodiles, crocodiles, crocodiles,
Snapping whenever I dream,
Nothing but crocodiles, save me from crocodiles,
Take them away or I'll scream.

Up and Up

When I climb to the top of the birch tree
I can see all the way to France,
I can see blue pigeons gliding down
To land on the Eiffel Tower.

When I climb to the top of the oak tree
I can see all the way to Greenland,
I can see fat, gap-toothed walruses
In battle with polar bears.

When I climb to the top of the beech tree
I can see all the way to China,
I can see a man called Ching Chai Ping
Pouring cups of bright-green tea.

When I climb to the top of the pine tree
I can see, if I screw up my eyes,
All the way round the world.

Sometimes I wave to myself.

Going to America

With sea-blue hats and sea-blue socks,
    Going to America,
We set sail in a cardboard box,
    Going to America,
The waves reared up and hid the sky,
    Going to America,
And sharks, as keen as knives, slid by,
    Going to America,
We rode the storm, we raced the gale,
    Going to America,
When, suddenly, up bulged a whale,
    Going to America,
The whale's tail slapped our skin-thin ship,
    Going to America,
And stove us in, and through the rip,
    Going to America,
Poured streaming seas, gushed freezing waves,
    Going to America,
Threatening us with watery graves,
    Going to America,
Land-ho! A wild coast loomed ahead,
    Going to America,
'Swim for your lives!' the Captain said,
    Going to America,

We dived, we swam, we fought our way,
    Going to America,
To the foot of a sheer cliff veiled in spray,
    Going to America,
And clinging on with teeth and nails,
    Going to America,
We climbed that cliff to search for sails,
    Going to America,
And when at last we reached the top,
    Going to America,
And balanced there, a voice cried, 'Stop!
How many times have I told you
Not to climb on the back of the sofa!'

The Rose and the Mole

'Leave off! Save me! Stop, please, stop!
I'm wriggling and giggling and laughing fit to drop.
I'm shaking all my petals off. Help!' cried the rose,
But the mole just kept on tickling her toes,
The mole kept tickling her toes.

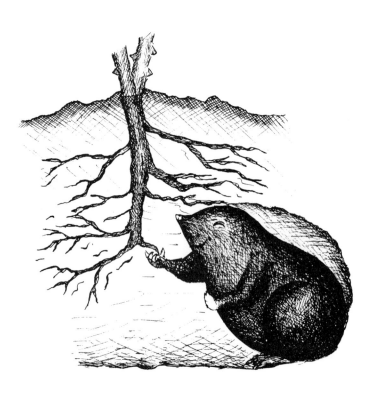

The Oddmedod

As I walked out one evening
On Under River Farm,
A tattered shape loomed through the mist
And caught and held my arm –
A scarecrow, old and ragged,
A withered, gasping thing,
A scarecrow made of sticks and straw
And rags tied on with string.

'No work no more for Oddmedods,
No place for us,' it said.
'Who needs an Oddmedod when there's
Them gun machines instead,
Them things that goes exploding
Enough to bust your brain,
While we're kicked out and left to rot
Under the freezing rain.'

The scarecrow coughed and rattled,
Loosening its grip of straw.
I freed my arm and ran,
And when I reached the gate, I saw
No Oddmedod behind me
At the field's misty edge,
Just sticks and straw and scraps of rag
Scattered in the hedge.

Alice and Elsa

Alice planned her garden:

It will have snowdrops and daffodils
And marigolds and honeysuckle
And roses that smell like soap.

It will have a pond with a mermaid.

It will have carrots in rows
And lettuces in clumps
And lots of strawberries.

It will have a greenhouse, tidy and warm,
Where my gardener will have his tea and biscuits
Out of the rain,

And it will have butterflies on the buddleia,
A robin on a spade
And hedgehogs at night, coming for milk.

Elsa planned her garden:

It will have thorn apples and toadstools
And hogweed and stinkwort
And a bed of deadly nightshade.

It will have a pond with a drowned ghost.

It will have knobbly squashes
And fiery peppers
And lots of quinces.

It will have a greenhouse, hot as a furnace,
Where my gardener will laze in her hammock,
Playing a pipe.

And it will have cougars in the trees,
Rattlesnakes in the rockery
And wolves at night, coming for meat.

Alice said to Elsa
You'll be welcome in my garden,
We can walk there together
On mild afternoons.

Elsa said to Alice
You'll be welcome in my garden,
We can walk there together
On white nights of lightning.

Asteroid Dog

I'm an asteroid dog,
And it's boring,
Hurtling through infinite space,
With no little green men I can play with,
And no little green cats I can chase.

I'm an asteroid dog,
And it's boring,
With nothing much better to do
Than watch the stars spin till I'm space sick –
And not even a slipper to chew!

I'm an asteroid dog,
And it's boring,
No rabbits, no alleys to prowl,
So I sit all alone on this cold lump of stone
And I howl and I howl and I howl
And I howl and I howl
And I howl and I howl
And I howl and I howl and . . .
I howl.

Poppies

'There are poppies in the barley,'
Said Susannah's farmer father.
'They're a nuisance. They contaminate the whole
    crop.
They're a curse.
I shall mix some good strong weedkiller
And drive down in the tractor,
And spray them till they burn away
Or next year they'll be worse.'

'There are poppies in the barley,'
Said Susannah to her father.
'They're like dancers dressed in papery red,
They dip, they nod, they sway.
If we run down there together
While the day's still warm and sunny,
We can watch them through the evening,'
But her father turned away.

The Spell

I've written a spell out on paper,
I've hidden the spell in a matchbox,
I've buried the spell in the garden,
I'm waiting for it to work.

★

The Beast didn't hit me this morning,
The Beast didn't hit me at lunch-time,
The Beast didn't hit me till swimming,
The spell is beginning to work.

★

The Beast wasn't there in assembly,
He's been in an accident, Dawn said,
I spent all of break in the playground,
The spell's going on with its work.

★

This morning they put up a notice,
He's broken his leg in three places,
I'm sorry. I'm not really sorry.
The spell has completed its work.

★

I've dug up the spell from the garden,
The writing's still clear on the paper,
I'm keeping it safe in its matchbox,
Just in case.

No Voles Here

No voles here,
Said the owls,
Deserting the silver fields.

No voles here,
Said the owls,
Floating along the hillside.

No voles here,
Said the owls,
Abandoning the moortop.

No voles here,
Said the owls,
Resting on the rim of a moon crater.

No voles here,
Said the owls,
Swerving round lightning on Jupiter.

No voles here,
Said the owls,
Beating past Saturn,
Fixing their gold eyes
Fiercely
On the stars.

Good Luck

I found a lucky four-leaved clover
Growing on a wall.
I climbed for it and slipped and, ouch!
Cracked three ribs in my fall.
Thank goodness for the clover
Or I might have cracked them all.

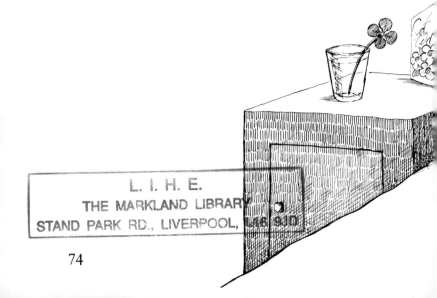

Index of First Lines